GET TO KNOW
YOUR PET

Hamsters and Gerbils

JINNY JOHNSON

A+

Smart Apple Media

Smart Apple Media is published by Black Rabbit Books
P.O. Box 3263, Mankato, Minnesota 56002

Printed in the United States of America

Johnson, Jinny.
    Hamsters and gerbils / Jinny Johnson.
    p. cm.—(Smart Apple Media. Get to know your pet)
    Includes index.
    Summary:"Describes the behavior of hamsters and gerbils
and how to choose and care for hamsters and gerbils as pets"—
Provided by publisher.
    ISBN 978-1-59920-092-7
    1. Hamsters as pets—Juvenile literature. 2. Gerbils as pets—
Juvenile literature. I. Title.
SF459.H3J65 2009
636.935'6—dc22

                                                2007052813

Designed by Guy Callaby
Edited by Mary-Jane Wilkins
Illustrations by Bill Donohoe
Picture research by Su Alexander

Thanks to Richard, James, Ella, Simon and Joe
for their help and advice

Picture acknowledgements
page 4, 5, 6, 7, 9, 11, 13, 14 & 16 Juniors Bildarchiv/OSF;
19 Imagebroker/Alamy; 22 E A Janes/RSPCA Photolibrary;
24 & 27 Juniors Bildarchiv/OSF
Front cover GK Hart/Vikki Hart/Getty Images

9 8 7 6 5 4 3 2

Contents

Hamsters–Wild and Tame

Hamsters are popular family pets. They are easy to look after, but they do need plenty of attention if they are to become friendly and tame.

Wild hamsters dig burrows where they shelter from the sun in the daytime. They usually come out at night to find food. Pet hamsters are quite happy to be left in peace during the day while you are at school. They like to wake up to play and eat during the evening.

HAMSTER FACT
Pet hamsters usually live for two to three years.

Wild hamsters feed mostly on seeds they find on the ground, but they eat some green plants too.

Hamster Characteristics

● A hamster is a rodent, like rats and mice.

● Hamsters have short legs and a tiny tail.

● Hamsters eat plant food, such as seeds, grain, fruit, and vegetables.

PET SUBJECT

Q Why does my hamster hide when I try to pick it up?

A In the wild, hamsters are prey animals. If a hamster sees something swooping down from above, such as your hand, it is frightened. It thinks it will be caught, so it tries to escape and hide. Let your hamster get to know your smell and don't try to grab it. Encourage it to be friendly by offering small food treats.

Types of Hamsters

Several types of hamsters can be kept as pets. Most popular is the Syrian hamster, also known as the golden hamster.

Syrian hamsters can be lots of different colors, including cream, white, and many shades of brown. There are also some long-haired varieties of Syrian hamster.

A Russian or dwarf hamster is smaller than a Syrian hamster. It is a very pretty little creature. Its coat may be brown, gray, white, or creamy colors. Chinese hamsters are slightly larger than dwarf hamsters and have a longer tail than other hamsters.

> **HAMSTER FACT**
> *Female hamsters can have several litters a year, each with six or seven babies.*

These little Russian hamsters like company. You can keep a pair together and they won't fight.

6

PET SUBJECT

Q Why does my hamster sleep so much?

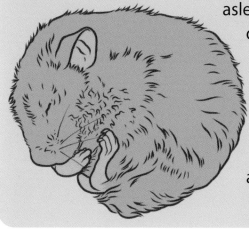

A Hamsters seem sleepy because they are nocturnal. That means they are usually active at night, perhaps when you are asleep. Wild hamsters prefer to come out at night when they are less likely to be caught by predators. Pet hamsters have the same habits. You will probably find your hamster is awake and ready to play in the evening if it has had a good sleep during the day.

Company—Or Not?

Syrian hamsters are happiest by themselves—that is how they live in the wild. They will fight if you try to keep them in pairs. Dwarf hamsters and Chinese hamsters live in groups in the wild. You can keep them in pairs or small groups of the same sex. Don't keep a boy and girl together, or you will end up with lots of babies.

Chinese hamsters have a longer tail than other hamsters and are sometimes called rat-tailed hamsters.

Choosing Your Hamster

Decide which kind of hamster you would like. You can buy several kinds in pet stores, but if you want a particular color or a special breed, you may need to go to a hamster breeder.

If you buy a hamster from a pet store, make sure the cages are clean and the animals look well cared for. You could also ask your local rescue center if they have any animals that need homes.

Both male and female Syrian hamsters make good pets. If you buy dwarf hamsters, you might prefer a female pair, as they are less likely to fight.

Many hamsters have sandy-colored fur. In the wild, this helps them stay hidden in their desert home.

What to Look For

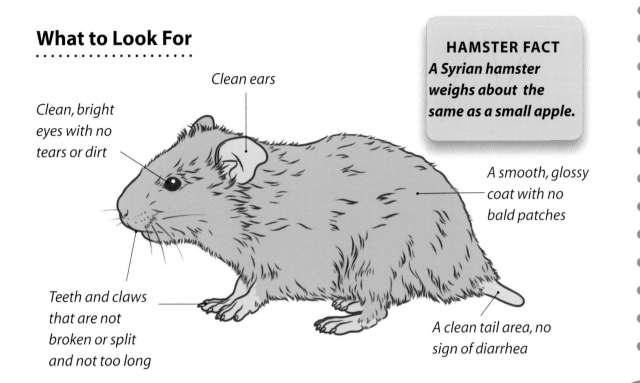

Clean ears

Clean, bright eyes with no tears or dirt

Teeth and claws that are not broken or split and not too long

A smooth, glossy coat with no bald patches

A clean tail area, no sign of diarrhea

9

PET SUBJECT

Q How well can hamsters see?

A Not very well. Hamsters have big bright eyes, but their eyesight isn't very good. Wild hamsters usually run around and feed at night. They rely on their sense of smell rather than sight to find food and avoid danger.

A Home for Your Hamster

Make sure you have everything ready for your hamster before you bring it home.

A Syrian hamster can live in a wire cage with a plastic base. It should be able to move around and exercise, so choose a large cage which measures at least 24 x 12 x 12 inches (60 x 30 x 30 cm).

Dwarf hamsters are smaller and could squeeze through the gaps in wire cages. A tank-style home with a wire lid is best for them. Again, choose a cage which measures at least 24 x 12 x 12 inches (60 x 30 x 30 cm) so they have plenty of space to run around.

Whatever cage you choose for your hamster, make sure it is safe and secure and has plenty of air.

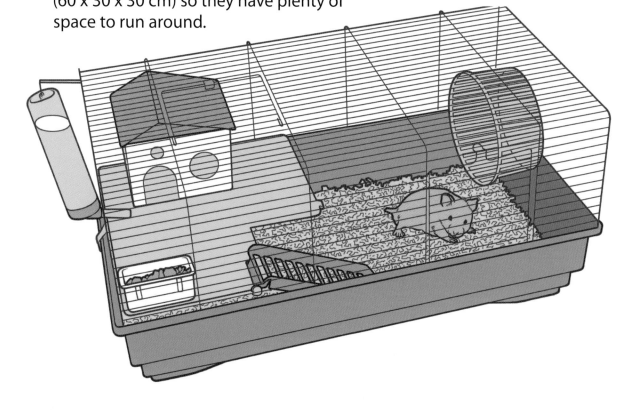

Preparing the Cage

Cover the base of the cage with something soft, such as wood shavings that have had the dust taken out. They soak up the hamster's pee. Hamsters can also be trained to pee in a jar, which helps to keep the cage cleaner. Your hamster will like something to burrow into, such as shredded paper or peat. Don't use fluffy bedding material, which can get tangled around a hamster's legs. Keep the cage away from drafts and direct heat or sun.

Your hamster will need food bowls, a water bottle that can be attached to the side of the cage, and some toys.

11

PET SUBJECT

Q Why does my hamster have such long front teeth?

A Hamsters have big front teeth so they can chew hard foods, such as seeds and nuts. A hamster's teeth keep growing all through its life, because if they became worn down, the animal wouldn't be able to eat. It's a good idea to give your hamster a chewing block so its teeth don't grow too long. You can buy these in pet stores.

Caring for Your Hamster

Your hamster will be scared when you first bring it home, so give it time to settle and get used to its new surroundings.

Make sure your hamster has all it needs, but don't handle it for the first few days. Then start putting your hand in the cage and letting your hamster have a sniff. Once it is used to you, encourage it to climb on to your hand, then scoop it up carefully. If you handle your hamster gently and regularly it will soon become tame.

Your hamster will love to ride on your hand once it gets to know you, but take great care not to drop it.

You can buy little woven beds called hamster nests to put in your hamster's cage. Some pets really enjoy a nap in one of these.

Always wash fresh food for your hamster. If you pick plants such as dandelions from the garden, make sure they haven't been sprayed with weedkiller.

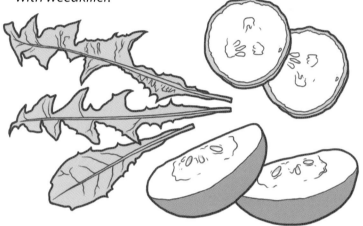

Feeding Time

Your pet needs special dried food for hamsters, which you can buy in pet stores. It will also enjoy small amounts of fresh food, such as pieces of apple and carrot. Your hamster will store food away, so check regularly for uneaten food, which may rot. Always make sure your hamster has clean water in a drinking bottle. Change the water every day.

PET SUBJECT

Q **Why does my hamster stuff food into its cheeks?**

A Wild hamsters use the pouches at the sides of the mouth to carry food back to their nests. They store food for times when there isn't much to eat. Pet hamsters don't need to do this, but it is part of their natural behavior. You may find lots of food stashed away in your hamster's bed or nesting box.

Hamster Fun

Hamsters are lively creatures and need to keep busy. But don't disturb your hamster during the day when it likes to sleep. It might bite you!

When your hamster wakes up in the evening, it will enjoy running through some cardboard tubes. Exercise wheels are also fun, but make sure you buy the solid kind. Hamsters can get their feet caught in wheels with spokes.

Many pet stores sell exercise balls for hamsters, but your pet may get very tired in one of these and find that it cannot get out. It's better to let your hamster run around in a safe place outside its cage. Take care though— hamsters move fast and can quickly scurry underneath furniture or out of sight.

Hamsters get lots of exercise in the wild as they look for food. An exercise wheel will help your pet keep active.

14

HAMSTER FACT
A Syrian hamster has four toes on each front foot and five toes on the back feet.

Grooming

Hamsters spend quite a lot of time grooming and they keep their fur in very good condition. If your hamster gets dirty when it's out of its cage, you could wipe it gently with a cotton ball moistened with warm water. Long-haired hamsters might need a gentle brush with a soft toothbrush if their fur becomes tangled.

A hamster often sits up on its back legs as it grooms itself.

Brush gently when you groom your hamster and keep the brush well away from its eyes.

PET SUBJECT

Q **Why does my hamster chew the bars of its cage?**

A Your hamster is probably bored and needs more to do. Make sure you give it plenty to play with inside its cage and some things to chew. A branch of a fruit tree is ideal for hamsters to climb on and to chew. Check that the tree hasn't been sprayed though. Try to give your hamster some attention every day and let it have some exercise outside its cage sometimes.

Gerbils–Wild and Tame

Gerbils are gentle little animals and fun to keep as pets. They live in groups in the wild, so they like company. They are happiest in groups of two or three.

Wild gerbils come from the deserts of Asia, where they live in underground burrows. They are very clean, and like many desert animals, they don't pee very much. This means they don't smell bad as long as you clean out their cage regularly.

GERBIL FACT
Pet gerbils live between two and four years.

Wild gerbils are sometimes known as sand rats or desert rats —perhaps because of their long tail.

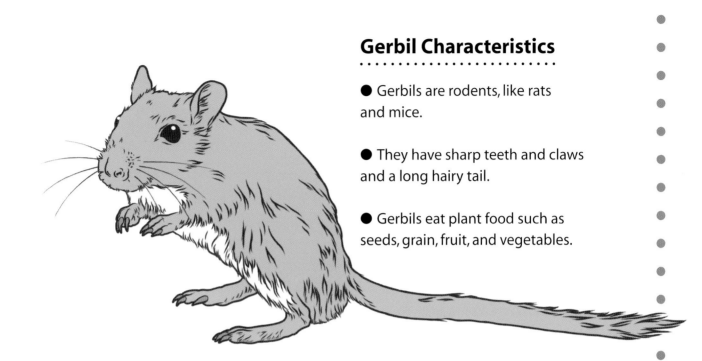

Gerbil Characteristics

● Gerbils are rodents, like rats and mice.

● They have sharp teeth and claws and a long hairy tail.

● Gerbils eat plant food such as seeds, grain, fruit, and vegetables.

17

PET SUBJECT

Q **Why does my gerbil rub its tummy on things?**

A It's spreading its own smell to mark its territory. Look at your gerbil's tummy and you will see a little patch of bare skin. This is its scent gland. It produces an oily liquid. Gerbils mark anything in their cage as well as each other with their scent.

Choosing Your Gerbils

You can buy gerbils from a pet store or a breeder. Make sure the animals are well cared for in good, clean cages.

Baby gerbils are usually ready to leave their moms when they are about five or six weeks old.

You can also get in touch with your local animal rescue center and find out if they have any gerbils that need homes. The gerbil usually sold as a pet is the Mongolian gerbil. There are many colors, including brown, gray, golden, cream, and black.

What to Look For

Choose a gerbil that is bright, lively, and inquisitive and not frightened when handled.

Clean nose, not runny.

Clean eyes.

Glossy coat.

Gerbils from the same litter get along well, but don't keep males and females together or you will have lots of babies.

PET SUBJECT

Q Do gerbils play together?

A Yes, pairs or groups of gerbils that live together will play and groom each other, which is great fun to watch. They often sleep cuddled up together in a heap.

A Home for Your Gerbils

Gerbils like to burrow in the wild, so your pets will be happiest if they can dig and tunnel in their cage.

A pair of gerbils needs a big cage measuring at least 16 x 30 x 12 inches (40 x 75 x 30 cm). Some gerbils are smaller and may be able to escape from wire cages, so a tank with a wire lid is best.

There are special cages for gerbils called gerbilariums. These have lots of plastic tubes making tunnels between different parts of the cage. This type looks fun, but gerbils can chew through thin plastic quickly. Whatever kind of cage you choose, make sure your pets have a nest box where they can hide away and sleep.

If you choose this type of cage, check often to make sure your gerbils haven't chewed holes in the tubes.

20

Preparing the Cage

Give your pets plenty of wood shavings to burrow in and some shredded paper for nesting. Gerbils also enjoy having a layer of peat to dig in.

Wild gerbils are burrowing animals, so make sure your gerbils have plenty of bedding to tunnel in.

PET SUBJECT

Q **How much water do gerbils need?**

A It's true that gerbils, like many desert animals, don't need a lot of water. But they do need some and should always have a water bottle in their cage with fresh water every day.

Caring for Your Gerbils

Gerbils are active at any time of the day and night. They usually sleep for a few hours, wake up for a while, and then take another nap.

Once gerbils get used to you, they will be happy to be stroked and picked up, but do this carefully and don't grab them or hold them by their tails.

Feed your pets a special dried food mix for gerbils and give them some fresh food every day. Apples, carrots, broccoli, and cauliflower are all good choices. Some gerbils like lettuce, but don't give them too much. Gerbils often hide food in their cage, so check and take any rotten food away. Gerbils like to have something to chew and you can buy wooden chew toys in pet stores.

Gerbils love fresh food as well as dried food, but too much fresh food can upset their tummies.

Picking Up Your Gerbil

Always approach your gerbil gently—don't make a sudden grab. Put one hand around its body behind its front legs, and support the back of the body with your other hand as you pick it up. Take care not to squeeze too hard. Never try to pick up a gerbil by its tail—it hurts!

PET SUBJECT

Q **Why does my gerbil bite me?**

A Gerbils don't usually bite, so perhaps your gerbil is frightened. When you put your hand in the cage, let your gerbils have a sniff and get used to your smell before you try to touch or stroke them. That way they won't be startled. Also, gerbils are curious little creatures and might just be trying to find out what this strange thing—your finger—is, in case it is good to eat.

Keeping in Touch

Hamsters and gerbils make squeaking sounds, although some of these are too high-pitched for us to hear.

They have other ways of sending messages to each other and us. Grooming and jumping around the cage are good signs and show that your pets are happy. A hamster that yawns and stretches as it wakes up is a happy hamster. But if your hamster walks with stiff legs, holds its ears back, or shows its teeth, it may be scared or upset and should not be disturbed.

These two dwarf Russian hamsters are sniffing each other to say hello.

PET SUBJECT

Q Why does my gerbil sit up on its back legs?

A It may be curious about something—you will see it sniffing the air and twitching its whiskers. But if your gerbil sits up with its front paws held together, it means it is frightened.

You will have lots of fun watching your gerbils playing together and greeting each other.

Gerbil Greeting

Gerbils often say hello by touching noses, but you may also see them licking each other's mouths. This is a way of greeting by checking the taste of the other animal. When a gerbil wants its friend to groom it, it may lie down and roll on its back.

GERBIL FACT
A gerbil is about 5 inches (12 cm) long and its tail is about the same length as its body.

Cleaning Out Your Pets' Cages

Hamsters and gerbils are clean animals, but they need your help to keep their cage tidy.

Every day, check your pets' cage and take out any uneaten food. Once a week, give the cage a thorough cleaning.

Put your hamster or gerbils in a safe place and throw out all the dirty bedding. Wash the base of the cage and any nest boxes and other items. Dry everything thoroughly and put in fresh bedding. Give the water bottle a good scrub too. If your gerbils' cage contains a layer of peat, this won't need changing as often.

Out of the Cage

Hamsters and gerbils enjoy running around outside their cages, but check that they will be safe first. They love to chew, so make sure they can't reach any electric wires or furniture legs. Watch out for poisonous plants too, and any other pets in the house. A bathroom can be a good place to start, particularly if it has a tiled floor. Keep your pets at floor level so they can't fall and hurt themselves.

PET SUBJECT

Q Why do gerbils like to roll in sand?

A Gerbils don't like water, but they do love a sand bath. In the desert, wild gerbils roll in sand to keep their fur clean and get rid of any greasiness on their coat. Your pet gerbils will love a dish of fine sand in their cage to roll in and clean themselves.

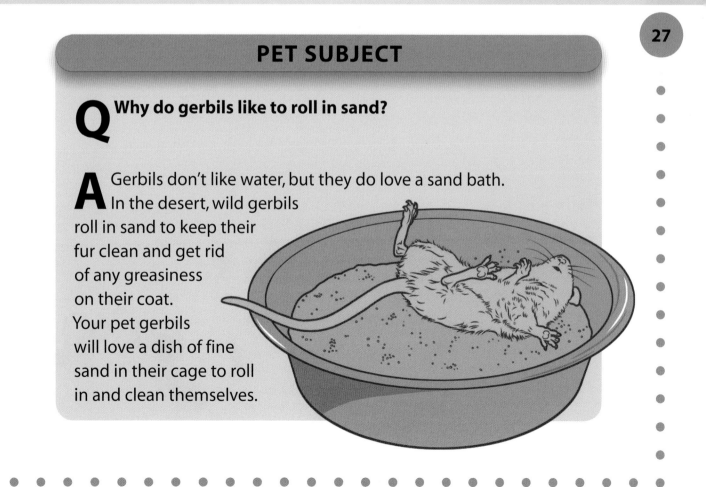

For Parents and Caregivers

Caring for any pet is a big responsibility. Looking after an animal takes time and money, and children cannot do everything themselves. You'll need to be prepared to show your children how to behave around the animal, provide what it needs, and make sure it is healthy. Once you have all the equipment, hamsters and gerbils don't cost a lot to look after and they don't need vaccinations.

Gerbils and hamsters are small creatures, but they may live for several years so you're taking on a big commitment. But helping to look after a pet and learning how to respect it and handle it gently is good for children and can be fun too.

CHOOSING AN ANIMAL

Make sure you choose a healthy animal. If you buy animals from a pet store, you might want to take them to the vet for a health check and advice on care.

Ask the vet to double check the sex of the animals too. Pet stores sometimes get it wrong! If you find your pet at a rescue center, it will have been checked already and they will give you lots of help with caring for and feeding your pet. When you've chosen your pet, you'll need a special carrier to bring it home. Hamsters and gerbils have sharp teeth and can chew their way out of a cardboard box in no time.

HOUSING

You'll need to have a cage and bedding ready for your pet or pets before you bring them home. They can be expensive. You'll also need to help your child clean out the cage regularly. Don't forget that these creatures may scurry about at night and may disturb children if kept in their rooms.

FEEDING

Once the pet is settled, a child can bring it dry food and change its water daily. Make sure you buy the right kind of dry food for your pet—hamsters and gerbils won't thrive on food that is for guinea pigs or rabbits. Children can give their pets fresh food too, but make sure they know what is safe and not safe for the animals and that they don't give them too much to eat.

HANDLING

It's very important to show your child how to handle a hamster or gerbil properly and that they learn that it is not a cuddly toy. These animals move fast and children may be tempted to squeeze them too tightly, which can hurt the animal. Teach your child to respect animals and always treat them gently.

Be very careful when you let your pet out of its cage—these small rodents can scuttle under furniture or hide in a tiny space in no time. Check the room carefully for escape holes or cracks before letting the animal out.

HEALTH CHECK

Check regularly for signs of parasites and make sure your pet's claws or teeth don't grow too long. Take your pet to the vet if its claws need clipping or if its teeth look overgrown.

Keep an eye on your pet's health and watch for any signs of illness. Hamsters can suffer from skin problems and tumors. Gerbils may also have allergies to bedding. Broken limbs are also common if pet animals have fallen in badly designed cages or if they have been handled roughly.

These small animals have short lives and your child will probably have to cope with the loss of the pet at some stage. Also, if a pet becomes seriously ill, you may need to explain to your child that it is kinder to ask the vet to put it to sleep rather than let it go on suffering.

Glossary

breeder
Someone who keeps hamsters or gerbils and sells the young they produce.

diarrhea
Very loose, runny poop.

grooming
Cleaning the fur.

litter
A group of young from the same mother.

mammals
A group of animals that includes dogs, cats, and humans, as well as hamsters and gerbils. Most mammals have four legs and some hair on the body. Female mammals feed their babies with milk from their own bodies.

nocturnal
Active at night. Nocturnal animals usually sleep during the day.

parasites
Tiny creatures such as fleas, lice, and mites, which can live on a hamster's or gerbil's body.

pouches
Pockets of skin in the cheeks where a hamster can store food.

predator
An animal that kills and eats other animals.

prey
Animals that are hunted and eaten by other animals.

rodents
A group of mammals that includes rats and mice as well as hamsters and gerbils.

scent gland
A special part of the body that makes a smelly liquid.

territory
An animal's home area where it spends most of its time.

Web Sites

For Kids:

ASPCA Animaland: Pet Care

http://www.aspca.org/site/PageServer?pagename=kids_pc_hamster_411

http://www.aspca.org/site/PageServer?pagename=kids_pc_gerbil_411

Sites for kids run by the American Society for the Prevention of Cruelty to Animals (ASPCA) with information on how to care for hamsters and gerbils.

Twin Squeaks Gerbils

http://www.twinsqueaks.com/index.php

A comprehensive site about Mongolian gerbils maintained by long-time gerbil owners.

Washington Humane Society: Caring for Hamsters

http://www.whs-kids.org/CompanionInfo/hamster.htm

A page for kids with essential information about hamsters.

For Teachers:

Best Friends Animal Society: Humane Education Classroom Resources

http://www.bestfriends.org/atthesanctuary/humaneeducation/classroomresources.cfm

Lesson plans and lots of information about treating animals humanely.

Education World Lesson Plans: Pet Week Lessons for Every Grade

http://www.educationworld.com/a_lesson/lesson/lesson311.shtml

Use the topic of pets to engage your students in math, language arts, life science, and art.

Lesson Plans: Responsible Pet Care

http://www.kindnews.org/teacher_zone/lesson_plans.asp

Lesson plans for grades preschool through sixth, covering language arts, social studies, math, science, and health.

Index